Working in Teams

James H. Shonk

Working in Teams

A Practical Manual for Improving Work Groups

amacom

A Division of American Management Associations

Library of Congress Cataloging in Publication Data

Shonk, James H.
  Working in teams.

  Includes index.
  1. Work groups—Management. I. Title.
HD66.S49   658.3'14   81-66238
                        AACR2

First Printing

To my parents
  Howard and Goldie Shonk

Preface

This book provides managers with the concepts and materials needed to develop and manage teams. It focuses on improving the team's ability to work together to accomplish its goals.

It is not a training program. It advocates a process to improve the team's effectiveness, a process that well-functioning teams often undertake as part of their regular work routine. It can be used as a complete guide to improve an existing team's performance, to start up a new team, or as a resource book for specific questions and answers. It is written for internal change agents as well as for managers.

The book has two premises. The first is that managers, given the appropriate guidance and materials, can effectively improve their teams' performance. Second, internal or external change agents can leverage their skills by training managers to accomplish many objectives for which they might otherwise seek outside help. The leverage comes from being able to train and provide materials for 10 to 20 managers or more within the same amount of time required to accomplish team development with one team.

To improve its effectiveness, a team must go through a development process. The steps in this process are depicted in the model on the facing page. This book will cover in detail each step in the team development process and explain the manager's role in implementation.

Acknowledgments

I am grateful to several friends whose contributions have made this book possible.

My associates at General Foods Corporation—Bill Bevans, Betty Duval, and Harry Montgomery—were very helpful during the early development and testing of the action materials. Dan Spurr reviewed and edited the first few chapters and helped to put some life into the prose. Ron Fry, a colleague with whom I have conducted several team development seminars, has provided stimulus as we have engaged in joint exploration and testing of the team development concepts that underlie the theoretical base of this book. I am grateful to Dick Beckhard for first developing the team development model on which this book is based, and for his help and counsel as we have worked together.

Margaret Oberdorster and Evelyn Helland have typed so many drafts and redrafts they have become experts in team development. Thank you, Mary Beth, my chief editor, critic, and supporter.

James H. Shonk

The Team Development Process

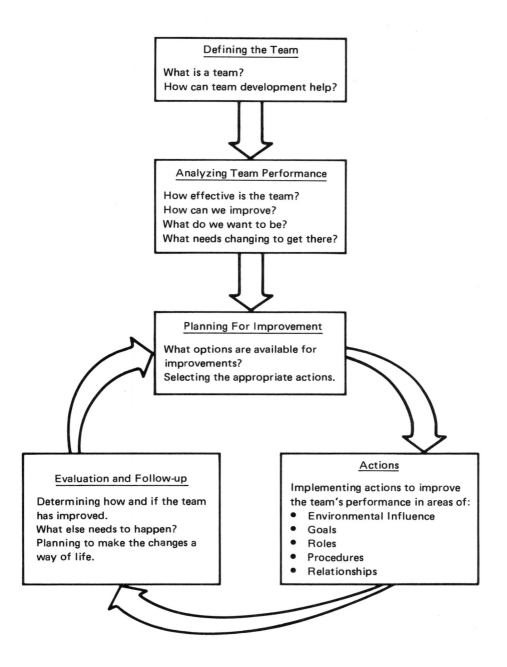

Defining the Team

What is a team?
How can team development help?

Analyzing Team Performance

How effective is the team?
How can we improve?
What do we want to be?
What needs changing to get there?

Planning For Improvement

What options are available for
improvements?
Selecting the appropriate actions.

Evaluation and Follow-up

Determining how and if the team
has improved.
What else needs to happen?
Planning to make the changes a
way of life.

Actions

Implementing actions to improve
the team's performance in areas of:
● Environmental Influence
● Goals
● Roles
● Procedures
● Relationships

Contents

1

What Is Team Development? Who Needs it?

Team development is the process of unifying a group of people with a common objective into an effectively functioning unit. In other words, it is the process of making a team truly productive.

Why Team Development?

The concept of teams of people working together is not a new phenomenon. Teams are in one way or another responsible for a large portion of an organization's output. The growing complexity of organizations in response to a multitude of changes in today's environment, such as expanding governmental regulations and accelerating technology, has increasingly resulted in their assembling people, with the many and diverse skills needed to respond to these demands, into work teams. Employees at all levels are at some point in their organizational life likely to be leaders or members of a team and will need to know how to effectively function within a team.

1

Although not a cure-all for an organization's ills, team development can improve the team's goal-setting skills, ability to establish clear responsibilities, decision making, communications, and interpersonal relationships to ultimately improve the team's contribution to the overall organization performance.

Defining the Team

A team consists of two or more people who must coordinate their activities to accomplish a common task.* It is not enough for people to *want* to coordinate because it would be nice. Coordination must be *required* to accomplish the task in order to justify setting up the team in the first place. If two people can best perform their work without coordination, they are not a team. If only a portion of their tasks requires coordination or interdependence, they are a team for only those tasks that require interdependence and coordination.

To be a team, members must be working toward a common task or a common goal—for example, the market introduction of a new product, or the design of a new manufacturing process. This does not mean that members of a team cannot have some independent goals, but if *all* their goals are independent, if there are no common goals toward which they are working, they are not a team. The *common goal* or task and the *coordination required* determine whether a team exists. Do they depend on each other's services to accomplish work? Make decisions jointly? Supply each other with resources? Sequence their efforts to accomplish an overall goal? Share a common resource? If the answer is yes, then it is likely that they are a team.

*Mark Plovnick, Ronald Fry, and Irwin Rubin. "New Developments in O.D. Technology: Programmed Team Development," *Training and Development Journal*, April 4, 1975.

A group of people may report to the same manager and still not be a team. For example, consider a group of project engineers in which each engineer is working on a different project for a different part of the organization, spending all his time on one project. His goals and interdependence with the other project engineers may be nil, and therefore the members of the project engineering group do not constitute a team. If members of this same engineering group are all working on one project, each doing a piece that will eventually fit together with other pieces or each requiring some of the talents of the others or making decisions that affect the others' work, they are very much a team.

As an example of a highly interdependent team reporting to the same manager, let us look at the manager of a manufacturing plant and his staff (Figure 1). A typical manufacturing plant usually has a production manager, financial manager, personnel manager, quality control manager, and an engineering manager. Each reports to the plant manager. These managers must continually coordinate their activities during a given day for the effective functioning of the manufacturing plant. Therefore, the plant manager and his staff are a team.

Employees at levels below the plant manager's staff who report to individual functional heads often have goals in common with peers who report to a different manager. Many of their activities and the accomplishment of their goals require coordination. Therefore, though they report to different bosses, they constitute a

Figure 1. Team reporting to same manager.

3

Figure 2. Team reporting to different managers.

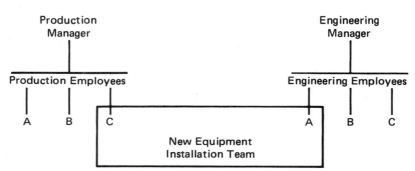

team when working on those tasks that require coordination. Figure 2 illustrates a team whose objective is to install a new piece of equipment on an existing manufacturing line. Production Employee C must coordinate with Engineering Employee A to install the equipment. Each has the same objective: equipment installation. They each have information and skills that must be coordinated to accomplish the task.

Teams can be permanent, with formal reporting relationships as in Figure 1. Members of permanent teams usually report to one manager and have ongoing organizational goals. Interdisciplinary teams, such as the plant manager's staff and the substaff, tend to be permanent. Temporary teams come together for a specific task and disband when it is completed. The members of a temporary team frequently have no formal or hierarchical reporting relationship. Task forces and project teams are usually temporary.

Teams vary in the extent of member interdependence and, therefore, in the amount of coordination required to accomplish tasks. To determine how much teamwork is needed or if a group of people constitute a team, you must first identify the goals or tasks to be accomplished and then examine to what extent the members are interdependent—that is, how great their need is to coordinate efforts to achieve their goals.

4

TEAM OR GROUP

The following questions will help you examine to what extent your group is interdependent and, therefore, to what extent it needs to function as a team. Circle the letter for the statement (A or B) that best describes your group or team and complete the examples.

I. *Goals*

    A. Members have common goals or tasks that require working together. Some common goals or tasks are:

    _____

    _____

    _____

    _____

    B. The goals and tasks of members are separate. Some goals/tasks that are separate or apply only to one member are:

    _____

    _____

    _____

    _____

II. *Interdependence*

    A. Actions or decisions of any one member impact upon the work of the other members. Some decisions/actions requiring involvement by or impacting upon two or more members are:

    _____

    _____

    _____

    _____

B. Members can make decisions or take actions without impacting upon the work of other members. Some decisions/actions that can be handled by one individual independent of other members are:

III. *Collaboration*

A. Work can be accomplished most effectively by members working together. Examples of work best accomplished through coordination are:

B. Members can accomplish their work most effectively by working alone. Examples of work best accomplished by members working alone are:

IV. *Time Frame*

    A. Activities must be coordinated on a daily/weekly basis. Examples of activities requiring frequent coordination are:

_____

_____

_____

_____

    B. Members can work for long periods of time, weeks/months, without coordinating activities with one another. Examples of activities that do not require frequent coordination are:

_____

_____

_____

_____

_____

    "A" responses indicate interdependence. The more "A" responses, the higher the interdependence of the team and the higher the need for teamwork. If your group fits none of the "A" responses, for the purposes of this book they are not a team and should not be concerned about trying to function as one. If members of a group are not interdependent and do not need to coordinate their activities, they will see little value in functioning more effectively together.

    Occasionally, teams operate as though they fit the "B" responses but should be working in the "A" response mode. It is probable that such a team is not working very effectively and could greatly benefit from team development.

2

Factors
That Influence
Team Effectiveness

To improve a team's effectiveness, it is first necessary to understand the factors that have impact on its performance. The materials in this chapter will lead to:

- Understanding what factors influence team performance and how these factors are related.
- Determining when team development is needed.

In order for teams to function effectively, they must manage how they work together and how they interact with the rest of the organization. As a result of his studies of teams, Richard Beckhard* postulates that teams, to be effective, must manage four areas that are internal to the team: goals, roles, processes, and relationships. These ideas have been further developed by Rubin, Plovnik,

*Richard Beckhard. "Optimizing Team Building Efforts," *Journal of Contemporary Business*, Summer 1972.

and Fry*, who determined that these variables are causally related. Ronald Fry and the author** have found that a fifth dimension to team life that must be managed is the team's interaction with its organizational environment. These five variables/areas become the focus of attention for the manager who wishes to improve team performance, because teams that effectively manage these areas will function more effectively than teams that do not. Each area and its causal relationships should be considered in detail.

Environmental Influences

The Impact of the Organization and the Outside World on Team Performance

All teams operate within a larger environment in the organization and ultimately in the outside world, which is most often represented by the marketplace. These outside influences have an impact upon the team and how it functions. Some common influences on team effectiveness are the organization's expectations of what the team should accomplish, the goals it defines for the team, the performance levels expected, the support given, the resources allocated, and so forth.

The organization creates the context within which the team functions. The policies, procedures, and systems within an organization can either support or hinder a team's effectiveness. An excellent example is the impact an organization's reward system has on teamwork.

*Irwin M. Rubin, Mark S. Plovnick, and Ronald C. Fry. *Task-Oriented Team Development.* New York: McGraw-Hill, 1978.
**Ronald C. Fry and James H. Shonk. Unpublished material developed for University of Michigan seminar on team development.

Organizations typically reward only individual contribution. Few organizations have found ways to reward teams. The result is that more attention is paid to individual performance.

Given an individual reward system, trade-offs may tend to be made in favor of individual effectiveness versus team effectiveness. To reinforce teamwork, one organization the author has worked with rewards individual performance through a merit pay system and team performance through a management bonus system. This has brought about a greater increase in teamwork within the organization than the many seminars on improving teamwork it has conducted. The seminars contributed to increased teamwork, but until the organization's reward system was changed to support teamwork, there were always driving forces in the form of rewards that were counter to the collaboration the firm was seeking.

Procedures for communicating organizational issues can also help or hinder a team's effectiveness. The communication system within an organization can be set up to keep all team members informed of matters that affect them, or to operate only through the established hierarchy, a process that may omit members of the team. It is common, particularly on cross-functional project teams, that some team members have not received important communications because they report to a supervisor who is one level below the supervisor to whom the other members report, and the lower level was not on the distribution list for that communication.

The organization structure may or may not be conducive to teamwork. A structure conducive to teamwork would organize teams of people around tasks that require coordination and interdependence and would provide appropriate support groups to which the team has access. Other criteria for organizing, such as administrative convenience, may be best for the organization but perhaps not conducive to building teams.

Goals—What the Team Is to Accomplish*

A team exists when members have responsibility for accomplishing a common goal. It is important that teams identify those tasks and goals that require interdependent action and those that do not, for members of a team will have individual goals that do not require coordination. An effective team is aware of and manages well the following:

The extent to which goals are clear, understood, and communicated to all team members. When each member is asked to identify the goals of the team, responses are often fairly consistent for the overall goal and usually involve making a profit or providing a service. However, one also finds that many divergent goals are advocated by team members. These differences in goal interpretation will lead each team member in a different direction and will usually result in much conflict and little teamwork.

The amount of ownership of team goals. It is important that members participate in setting team goals and that they are committed to them. If goals are mandated from the top, team members should have an opportunity to determine how they will be accomplished. The degree of goal ownership and the amount of energy expended toward reaching goals are to a great extent determined by the amount of participation in creating them and determining how they will be accomplished.

The extent to which goals are operational. Goals should be well defined, quantified if possible, and specific enough that members will know when they have accomplished them and can measure the result.

The extent to which goals are shared. On many teams, members do not share their goals with one another. Therefore, it is not clearly understood by all members

*This and the next three sections are adapted from *Task-Oriented Team Development* by Rubin, Plovnick, and Fry.

what others are trying to accomplish, the possible impact upon them, and how their actions can help or hinder. During a meeting with a company president and his staff in one of the author's client systems, the financial manager was sharing his goals with the team. This was the first time this team had shared the goals they each had set in one-on-one meetings with the president. The marketing manager was horrified when the financial manager mentioned that he was cutting two financial analysts from his organization in order to cut costs. The marketing manager had made a commitment to do much more financial analysis of business proposals to correct some poorly analyzed decisions made the year before. If this sharing of goals had not taken place, the financial analysts who were to provide assistance to the marketing manager may not have been available when he needed them.

The extent of goal conflict. Occasionally, the goals of team members will be in conflict. In the previously mentioned example, the financial manager's goal was to cut costs by eliminating two financial analysts, whereas the marketing manager's goal was to improve the quality of marketing decisions through more and better financial analysis. Both had reviewed their goals with the president but did not discover the conflict until they met to share and discuss individual and team goals.

Roles—Who Does What on the Team

Following effective goal management, the next major issue the team must manage is, Who is going to do what? or, What are our roles? Issues that teams need to manage relative to roles are:

Role clarity. Do all members understand what they and others are to do to accomplish the task? Do they know their individual responsibilities and limits of authority? It is common in the author's work for members of teams to say that they know what their roles are, especially if the team has been working together for some time. This is not true of new teams where roles are still being defined. However, in established teams considerable difference can exist in the way a member perceives his role and how another member of the team perceives it. As they work together, members also build expectations of one another that are seldom recorded in job descriptions or other organizational documents. These expectations should be discussed and agreed upon, as they greatly determine team members' roles.

Role conflict. Do members' roles complement one another or are they in conflict? Conflict over roles may occur as a result of differing expectations among team members. Overlapping roles can create conflict, especially when two or more members see themselves as responsible for the same task. Staff and line positions on a team often have overlapping responsibilities. For example, who is responsible for hiring an employee? Is it the responsibility of the line manager, of the personnel manager, or of both? If it is the responsibility of both, what parts of the hiring process are performed by the line manager, and what by the personnel manager? Role overlaps are not inherently bad. However, overlaps and the reasons they exist need to be clearly understood. As long as an overlap exists, there is the potential for conflict. Occasionally, members of a team will not accept or agree with a role that has been defined for them by others. This occurs most frequently when a new member of a team does not view his role in the same way as his predecessor.

Work Processes—How Members Work Together

Now that team members know *what* they are to do and *who* is to do it, they must determine *how* they will work together. It is at this point that issues of *work process* are examined, that is, *how* the team will function as it accomplishes its task. These issues are:

Decision making. The most common issue among teams concerns decision making. Who is responsible for the decisions and how each of the team members participates in the decision must be clearly defined so that decisions are of high quality and are accepted by the members. Typically, two or more members may feel that they are responsible for the decision, and a conflict ensues about who should make it. When this occurs, it is often not an either/or situation, but one in which both parties have a contribution to make in reaching the decision. Occasionally, no one on the team feels responsible for the decision, so no decision is made.

Communications. What should be communicated within the team, to whom, by what method, when, and how frequently? When it is found that team members do not communicate with each other as much as they should, the "pendulum" reaction is to communicate everything to everybody, and then team members, of course, feel overwhelmed. Effective team communication requires that the team manage the optimum level of communication, the method, and the timing among team members and between the team and the outside environment.

Meetings. If you were to conduct an informal poll of team members and friends and ask them whether they are satisfied with the team meetings they attend, you may find that a substantial number of them believe team meetings are ineffective, dull, repetitive, too long, too frequent, cover the wrong subjects, are dominated by a few people, or seem a waste of time. The questions to be resolved concerning meetings are:

1. What is the team trying to accomplish in this meeting?
2. What subjects are to be covered in the meeting?

3. Who is responsible for the subject?
4. How will the meeting be conducted?
5. Who should attend?

Leadership style. The leadership style employed by the manager greatly affects the team's communications, decision making, and work processes. The author has consulted with effective team leaders who are authoritarian and with others who are participative. The leader and the team should examine the situation and determine the most appropriate style. The intent of this book is not to change the manager's style but, it is hoped, to alert him to the need to frequently examine the impact of his style on the team and to be open to feedback from team members regarding how that style contributes to or detracts from the team's effectiveness.

Relationships—The Quality of Interaction Among Team Members

As team members work together, relationships often become strained. Members need ways to resolve problems and to assure that a good working relationship continues. Sometimes relationship problems occur because of a difference in values or a personality or management style clash.

A team member's feelings, attitudes, and emotions can greatly affect personal relationships and the team's ultimate effectiveness. The more energy that is syphoned off because of bad feelings, attitudes, or strong emotions, the less energy is available for the team's task.

Occasionally an intrapersonal issue will arise; for example, a person may simply not like working in a team setting or may not like or be suited for the type of work the team is performing. Such issues usually require conversation between the manager and the person. To salvage the relationship, the manager must help the person adjust or, if this is not possible, find the person a job that better suits him.

We may summarize the factors influencing team effectiveness as follows:

Environmental Influence—The Impact of Influences Outside of the Team
    Policies and procedures.
    Systems: rewards and communications.
    Organization structure.
    Outside demands: customers and government.

Goals—What the Team Is to Accomplish
    Understanding and need for clarity.
    Ownership and agreement.
    Operational: specific and measurable.
    Shared among team members.
    No conflicts.

Roles—Who Does What
    Understanding and need for clarity.
    Agreement and ownership.
    No conflicts.

Processes—The Way in Which the Team Accomplishes Work
    Decision making.
    Communications.
    Meetings.
    Style of leadership.

Relationships—Quality of Interaction
    Interpersonal conflicts.
    Feelings/attitudes/emotions.
    Intrapersonal issues.

Hierarchy

Rubin, Fry, and Plovnick* found that these variables interact, that poor or good performance in one area can affect another. Furthermore, they found that there is a hierarchy of interaction for these variables.

Some variables were found to potentially influence all others. Those at the top of the hierarchy influence all below them. The team hierarchy can be depicted as follows:

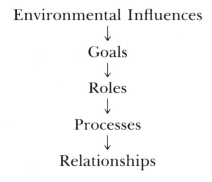

Environmental Influences
↓
Goals
↓
Roles
↓
Processes
↓
Relationships

This interactive influence can be illustrated by examples of problems commonly identified by teams and by examining the root causes of the problems. For example, requests for team development activity often start with two members of the team feeling they have a relationship problem. Experience has shown that often these members do not have a relationship problem outside of work; that is, they socialize well outside of the workplace. Closer examination reveals the root of the relationship problem is that they disagree on what the goal should be for the team, or they have conflicting roles, or one thinks the team should make decisions as a group and the other

*Irwin M. Rubin, Ronald C. Fry, and Mark S. Plovnick. *Managing Human Resources in Health Care Organizations: An Applied Approach.* Reston, Va.: Reston Publishing Co. Inc., 1978.

17

that each person should make decisions in his own area of responsibility. What appears to be a relationship problem may have another root cause and may in fact be a goal, role, or process issue.

Environmental influences sometimes put different and conflicting demands on members of the team and can create relationship problems. On a multidisciplined project team, where members report to different functional heads, the conflicting demands of the two bosses may lead to team conflict, which is manifested and diagnosed as a relationship problem. The root cause, however, is the conflicting multiple demands from the outside environment.

When one member of a team sees the goal as X and another sees it as Y, it becomes obvious why they always argue during team meetings. Properly diagnosed, this is a goal problem, and if the manager attempts to solve it by improving the relationship between the two parties, he is working at the wrong level of the team hierarchy. Similarly, role problems may be the result of poor understanding or definition of the goal.

Therefore, what appears to be a problem at one level of the hierarchy may have its root cause at a higher level. When in doubt as to where the problem exists, first look at the higher-level variables to determine what, in fact, is causing the problem, before you attempt to solve the problem at the level where the symptoms first appear.

When Team Development Is Needed

Over the past three years, the author has collected data during public seminars on team development, as well as from several business, health, and governmental organizations. Line managers, personnel managers, outside consultants, and internal consultants were asked the following question: What are the characteristics of teams that are functioning well or poorly? Responses to this question were cataloged, using the team hierarchy. In the vast majority, items fell under one of the five areas of the hierarchy. A sample array of responses follows.

CHARACTERISTICS OF TEAMS

Well-Functioning Teams	Poorly Functioning Teams
Environmental Influences	*Environmental Influences*
1. Team members are in close physical proximity and able to meet regularly.	1. Physical separation prevents members from meeting frequently.
2. The appropriate skills are represented on the team.	2. Team is not given adequate resources to do the job.
3. The appropriate levels of organizational authority are present within the team.	3. There is no recognition of team effort.
	4. There is a lack of recognition by the organization or its leaders that a team exists.
Goals	*Goals*
1. Team members are involved in the setting of objectives.	1. Members do not participate in setting goals.
2. Objectives are understood by all members.	2. Goals are unclear.
3. All individuals agree with objectives.	3. Goals are not communicated.
4. Objectives are set and met within realistic time frames.	4. Everyone is doing his own thing without attention to team goals.

Well-Functioning Teams	Poorly Functioning Teams
Roles	*Roles*
1. Roles are clearly defined and do not overlap.	1. Responsibilities are poorly defined.
2. Team members and their leader know their assignments.	2. No clear leader is identified.
3. Roles are understood by all and are supported.	3. There is buck-passing of responsibility.
4. There is strong, effective leadership with clearly defined responsibilities.	4. Members engage in power plays for authority and control.
5. Members and the leaders are accessible to help each other.	5. Members refuse to recognize their interdependence and act as if they were independent.
Procedures	*Procedures*
1. Decisions are made by consensus.	1. Decisions are always a crisis situation.
2. Meetings are efficient and task-improvement oriented.	2. Decision making is dominated by one person.
3. Emphasis is on solving problems, versus blaming the individual responsible for the problem.	3. Communications are one way —from top down—and channeled through the leader.
4. All members participate in discussions and meetings.	4. Minor points are debated endlessly.
5. Minutes of meetings are promptly distributed.	5. Meetings are unproductive with the issues unresolved.
6. Members listen well.	6. Meetings cover trivia, versus significant issues.
7. There is frequent feedback to individuals regarding performance.	7. Actions are taken without planning.
8. All members are kept informed.	8. Members work individually and ignore each other.
9. Deadlines and milestones are clearly established and agreed to by team.	9. Members are late for meetings or do not attend.

Well-Functioning Teams	Poorly Functioning Teams
Relationships	*Relationships*
1. There is team identity or esprit de corps and pride.	1. Members are unwilling to be identified with the team.
2. There is tolerance for conflict, with an emphasis upon resolution.	2. There is covert conflict between members.
3. Conflict is openly discussed, often resulting in growth or learning.	3. There are severe personality conflicts.
4. Members enjoy each other.	4. Relationships are competitive.
5. Team members support each other.	5. Members are defensive.

If your team resembles that characterized under the right-hand column, it is a prime candidate for team development. If your team is similar to that characterized under the left-hand column, it probably does not need team development. Very likely your team is not a pure prototype of either of these but has characteristics from both.

New Teams

Team development is often helpful when new teams are formed. The team hierarchy can serve as a road map for the new team to follow to ensure that it gets off on the right foot. In addition, new situations that cannot be classified as productive or unproductive often call for some type of team development. They might involve a new boss, new team members, new team responsibilities, or a newly reorganized team or department.

21

Team Development

Team development is a process whose ultimate goal is to improve a team's performance in any one or all of the five areas in the team hierarchy. After examining your team's performance in these areas, you must decide whether team development can be an effective tool for improving its performance. Methods to be used in examining your team's performance will be outlined in Chapter 3.

3

Starting a Team Development Effort

The manager and the team members should review a number of considerations before starting a team development effort. This chapter will provide the materials for the following:

- Review of prerequisites to effective team development and any needed corrective action.
- Review of risks associated with team development and actions needed to reduce them.
- Determining whether to use a consultant.
- Deciding whether to proceed or not.
- Introducing team development to the team.

Prerequisites for Team Development

Prior to entering into team development, a manager must consider a number of prerequisites, much as a pilot reviews a checklist before takeoff to ensure a smooth flight. For the most fruitful team development, the following prerequisites should apply to the team:

1. *The group being considered is interdependent,* or is, in fact, a team as discussed in Chapter 1. If members are not interdependent, that is, do not need to coordinate their activities, there is little value in team development for the group.

2. *Team members believe there are significant areas that need to be improved* and that team development can help. If members think the issues are not significant, the team development effort is likely to be done in a perfunctory manner with little motivation or commitment to making effective change.

3. *The motivation for change comes from within* the team, the team can see the need for change, and the advantage of changing can be clearly identified. If the pressure for change is external to the team, the team's commitment and follow-through and the resultant change will be less than desired.

4. *The team has power to do something about the issues* identified for improvement. If all or a few key issues lie outside the team's sphere of influence, perhaps the manager and/or other members of the organization should resolve them before the team looks at its own performance. The manager should be cautioned that team members may use this to delay or permanently postpone team development activities. It is important that the team understand there will always be issues outside its influence that will have impact on its performance. In addition, there will always be issues within the team's sphere of influence that it has an opportunity to change in order to improve. It is a matter of weighing these two to ensure that the external influences are not so great that the team feels little motivation to move ahead on its own. It is often necessary for the team to resolve internal problems

so as to build its solidarity and ability to confront and solve external problems.

5. *Team members are willing to risk new ways of working together.* The manager must accept the fact that the way he is presently managing may need to be changed for more effective functioning of the team. Team members must be willing to accept new modes of management and new methods of relating to the manager and fellow team members. This willingness to try new behaviors also requires an acceptance by all team members that they, in fact, may contribute to the team's ineffectiveness or be a part of the problem or solution. If team members are convinced that all problems are caused solely by someone other than themselves and that they do not need to change, there will, at best, be a very shaky foundation for a team development effort. If all the team members are willing to examine their behavior and make conscious choices about how they can change and therefore improve the team's effectiveness, they are building the essential and firm foundation for a fruitful team development effort.

6. *Tangible short-term results* can be accomplished through team development efforts. This does not mean that long-term efforts should not be undertaken, for, in fact, team development takes time. Depending on the number of issues and their complexity, team development typically happens over a three- to six-month time span. It is expected that a team starting a development effort will look for successes, and short-term success is not only the place to start but the prerequisite to a successful long-term development effort.

7. *Team members are willing to do a real diagnosis* or examination of how the team functions at present to determine what might be creating problems for the team and what the options are for improvement. This diagnosis must incorporate all members' views. The process of so-

25

liciting all points of view also helps to build everyone's commitment to team development. Accepting a hurried diagnosis or one person's view of the problem does not save time but, rather, may result in a loss, causing low commitment by team members or perhaps misidentification of the issues.

8. *All team members accept that feelings and attitudes are important* in determining how a team functions. There will be times in a team development effort when team members will not be able to express explicitly what they feel is inhibiting the team's progress. They may only have a feeling about what the problem is or they may have attitudes that inhibit their own effectiveness as a team member. Although the prime focus is the task upon which the team is working, one must not forget the human element and the importance of feelings, emotions, and attitudes in work performances.

Obviously, all these prerequisites do not have to be met 100 percent to proceed with a team development effort. However, if some of them are not met, the manager should carefully consider the value of proceeding. Careful prework and planning by the manager can often fill a prerequisite gap. For example, to increase the team's motivation for change, the manager can help members identify the advantages of team development and understand what is involved in such an effort. It is best to go slowly at first and have as much discussion as necessary to ensure that team members understand and support the development effort.

Risks

Most team development projects get under way with some discussion of the potential disadvantages. Team members are typically concerned about discussing how they see the team functioning and how others contribute to the team's effectiveness or ineffectiveness. This concern often emanates from experiences with unstructured approaches to team development where members discuss their feelings and attitudes about other members and how they affect the working life of the team. This approach can at times be helpful but may also be very threatening. Team members' feelings and attitudes about each other are important to the team's functioning but should be discussed within the context of how they affect the accomplishment of the task and in a way that is constructive and productive.

In the *task-focused* approach to team development, which the author advocates, members talk about how they work together to accomplish a task and what members might do to improve the overall effectiveness of their working together. This type of discussion makes it considerably easier for members to express their concerns, because the *primary focus is on what is needed to better accomplish the team's tasks* and not on how individuals should change.

The discussion of potential risks is an important step in that it begins to establish the ground rules for the team development effort. The understanding that the focus will be on the team tasks usually relieves some apprehensions and frees up energies for the development effort.

Multilevel Team Development

As a general rule, team development should be done with only two levels of organization members composing the team, a leader and his team members. Most teams have a leader, either formally appointed or informally emerging from the group. The manager Level I and his team members Level II would make up a typical team, for example, Team A.

There may be occasions when the "two levels only"

concept may not be applicable. Doing team development with more than two levels (see Figure 3)—that is, a manager Level I, a subordinate Level II, and that person's subordinates Level III—presents certain difficulties. There is always a person who is in the middle. When a Level III person makes comments about a Level II person's performance with the Level I boss present, it is often uncomfortable for all and difficult to discuss.

The opportunity always exists for subordinates to use such a forum to put their manager on the carpet with the boss. Or subordinates may feel constrained about speaking up because they have a fear of putting their boss in a tough spot.

Team development with three levels requires a high level of trust among the members. If team development must include more than two levels, it is best to proceed with the leader (Level I) and the team members (Level II) first, and then have the Level II team members initiate

Figure 3. Multilevel team.

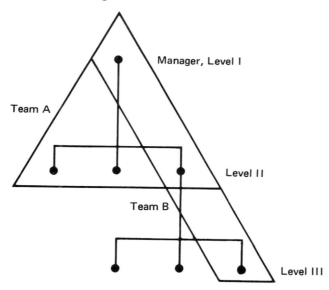

team development activities with their team members (Level III).

Sometimes in working with cross-functional teams neither the leader nor the two-level rule can be applied. If there is no leader, there must be someone who feels responsible for the functions that the leader usually undertakes in a team development effort—pulling the team together, seeing that decisions are made, and seeing that follow-up takes place.

If more than two levels of management are involved, a clear agreement must be reached prior to team development meetings about how issues identified in the session will be solved, whether they are to be solved between a manager and his subordinates or with all three levels involved.

Using a Consultant: Yes or No?

The materials in this book are designed so a manager and the team can use them without the aid of a consultant. The idea for this book and the self-administration concept of team development first occurred to the author while reading an article on consultant-free team building. Gibb and his associates, after experimenting with team building without the use of consultants, drew the following conclusions from their study:

Managers who plan and conduct their own meetings without a consultant present tend to see the meetings as more productive and useful than do comparable managers who use consultants to help plan and conduct the meetings.

Team-building meetings that focus on the solution of operating problems seem to be more effective in improving team effectiveness than do meetings that focus more directly upon process and personal issues. There seems to be little question that the integration of process and interpersonal data into work is necessary and useful. Hidden and latent process and interpersonal issues reduce effectiveness. The critical issue has to do with how this integration takes place.

The fact that a team agrees to get together for a sustained period of uninterrupted time to work together on crucial operating problems seems, in itself, to be a powerful organizational intervention.

One of the positive effects of consultantless team development is that managers get a new appreciation of their competence and power, their ability to do things on their own, and their ability to influence the system. The chronic assumptions by management and professional consultants about the consultant role tend to increase the manager's dependency and passivity.

One way of changing one's own attitudes about the effectiveness of teams is to have a powerful and successful experience with effective team management. Managers who learn to build an effective team increase their confidence in themselves and in the team; fears are reduced; constraints become less powerful; creativity is increased.

The role of the consultant (inside or outside the company) in such a program is to continue to reinforce the efforts of the line manager to be proactive, assertive, interdependent, and to take responsibility for his own operations. The consultant continues to take less responsibility, give less advice, give up more functions, and work himself out of a job more quickly than the manager wants him to. As the consultant begins to take a more personal, open, allowing, and interdependent stance, he becomes more effective in reducing dependency-passivity in the line managers with whom he works.*

Managers feel they need a consultant more frequently than they actually do. A few situations in which consultants seem to be most needed are:

---

*Jack R. Gibb. "TORI Theory: Consultantless Team Building," *Journal of Contemporary Business*, Summer 1972.

1. When the manager's style of management is a major contributor to the team's problems.
2. When there are major conflicts or relationship problems that require an impartial third party facilitator.
3. When nonproductive patterns of behavior and team norms have been reinforced over a long period of time and are, therefore, hard to change and often not challenged by the work group.

While conducting team development meetings, managers may feel that managing and contributing to the team decisions and monitoring the group's process is too much for them to handle. A *process guide* to help the manager and the team monitor its own process and thereby take some of the pressure off the manager will be discussed further in Chapter 6.

Guidelines for Using a Consultant

If you feel that your team fits one of the situations in the preceding list and you choose to use a consultant, either someone in your organization who serves in a staff-helping role or an external consultant, some guidelines will help you determine the best working arrangement. The most important issue in working with a consultant is to clearly define the roles of the consultant and the manager. The *manager should manage the team development effort;* that is, he is responsible for running the meetings, for seeing that decisions are made, and for seeing that follow-up takes place. The *consultant's role is to help the manager plan the team development activity.* If necessary, the consultant can help to ensure that listening takes place between team members and that good group process is followed. The consultant should also bring technology in the form of expertise, materials, and exercises to work on specific problems that have been identified by the team.

It is imperative that the manager and consultant develop a mutually comfortable working relationship. For the consultant to be helpful, the manager must be willing to confide in him. The manager needs to feel that the consultant is committed to the success of the team development effort. Early in the work relationship they should discuss what each expects of the other as they work together. The manager should expect the consultant to clarify how he will use data they are collecting, not usurp the manager's role, and indicate when he can or cannot be helpful in a situation. The manager should expect the consultant to bring ideas, concepts, options, materials, and technology that can be helpful to the team. The consultant should expect the manager to keep him informed of important developments, frankly discuss concerns and plans, and give feedback about why he accepts or rejects ideas. During the life of the relationship, they should regularly exchange feedback about the pluses or minuses of working together and how to improve the relationship.

The agreement between the consultant and the manager is typically called a contract. It should be written to ensure mutual understanding and should be renewable by either party. Mutual agreement is needed to change the contract. Either party should be able to terminate the contract whenever he believes the working relationship is no longer productive. However, termination should not take place without a discussion in which both parties understand and agree to the reasons for the termination. This prevents the sort of misunderstanding that often occurs when one of the parties undertakes an activity that the other does not understand or agree with. Discussion of the reasons for the activity may change the mind and alleviate the concerns of either party. Co-planning by the manager and consultant should help to prevent this problem from occurring.

Decision to Proceed

The manager, after reviewing the prerequisites for undertaking team development and after deciding to go ahead with such an effort, then must review the matter with the team. At this point, the decision to go ahead with team development is usually made in the same manner that the manager and his team make other decisions but with one qualification. If the manager usually makes a unilateral decision, he can expect less commitment than desired from team members in the team development process. Therefore, the decision to do team development requires at a minimum holding a meeting to solicit the team members' opinions as to whether they wish to start a team development activity. He should express a positive point of view regarding his reasons for team development, solicit the thoughts of his subordinates, and be alert to their concerns. The manager should be open to the influence of others and encourage others to state their views.

Introducing Team Development

As a manager, in talking with the team, you should:

1. Review the team development guide to explain what it is and what the outcome might be.
2. Express your reasons for wanting to do team development.
3. Discuss what you believe the outcomes would be.

4. Ask the group for opinions regarding the need for team development.

5. Answer team members' questions or concerns.

It is likely that some members will want to push ahead with team development, some may be uncertain, and others may be reluctant. The manager should be open to *not* proceeding if enough people express strong reservations. It is not unusual for some people to be somewhat concerned about proceeding with team development, because it involves unknowns and may result in changes for them. It may be necessary to spend additional time with these people to help them see the advantage of proceeding. Provided resistance is not overwhelming, the manager may need to decide that he will proceed with the team development efforts even though one or two members of the staff may be hesitant. If so, he must be aware of the implications of resistance and lack of commitment among members who don't agree to do team development. The author does not believe it is necessary to have unanimous agreement prior to engaging in team development, for unanimity may never be reached. Waiting for unanimous agreement assumes that the team can make such a decision when, in fact, decision making may be one of the issues the team needs to work on. The optimum situation, of course, is unanimous agreement, and the manager should allow enough discussion to reach the optimum if it is attainable.

TEAM DEVELOPMENT GUIDE

Definition and Purpose

Team development is any planned activity that helps to improve the operating effectiveness of a work team and its ability to resolve the issues that arise as team members work together. This is usually done by examining how the team functions at present in five general areas:

1. *Environmental influences*—The impact of influences outside of the team on its performance, for example, policies, procedures, systems, organization structure, customers.

2. *Goals/objectives/mission* (what the team does)—How are they set? Are they clear? Are they agreed to? Is there commitment? Are they operational? In conflict?

3. *Roles* (who does what)—Are roles clearly defined? Does everyone know what others expect of him? Do roles overlap or conflict?

4. *Procedures* (how the team accomplishes work)—How effectively the group is working, such as the effectiveness of meetings, decision making, communications.

5. *Relationships* (how members relate to one another)—The work relationships among the members and their impact on the team's effectiveness.

The Team Development Process

The team examines how it is functioning for the purpose of improving its working effectiveness. The process used includes the following:

1. Areas for improvement are solicited from the team members by questionnaire.
2. The results are presented anonymously to the manager who prepares a summary for the team to review.
3. The team reviews the information, decides which issues will be selected for further work, and determines their priority.
4. Plans are developed by the manager with the help of the team members to work on the issues identified.

35

Outcomes

Depending upon the focus, the outcomes of team development might be:

1. Identification of how the team is interdependent and what issues do or do not require close coordination by team members.
2. Improvement of the team's interaction with its environment.
3. Clearer goals with less conflict and more commitment to them.
4. Clarification of team members' roles and responsibilities.
5. Improvement in the procedures the team uses to accomplish its work, such as decision making, communications, and meetings.
6. Identification of unproductive work relationships with solutions and commitments to try more productive modes of working together.
7. Better solutions than would be arrived at by individuals and higher team commitment to them.

4

Analyzing
Team Performance

All members complete a questionnaire to determine how effectively the team is performing. The manager reviews the results and then reviews them with the team to determine the strong points of the team, areas for improvement, and their priority. Completing this section of the team development process provides a clearer picture of how the team is functioning and achieves agreement by the team of what needs to be improved. The sequence of events in this analysis is as follows:

- Manager reviews questionnaire with team to inform members about data to be collected and how they will be used and answers questions. Requires about 20 minutes.
- All team members including manager complete questionnaire in 45 minutes.
- Questionnaire is sent to central location for summarizing.

- Manager reviews questionnaire summary to plan for data feedback meeting. Requires one to two hours.
- Summary and analysis of key issues are sent to team members to individually identify issues and priorities. Time alloted: one to two hours.
- Manager leads joint data feedback meeting to gain understanding of issues, establish priorities, and determine first steps. Meeting requires two to four hours.

Questionnaire or Interviews?

After agreement has been reached to proceed with the team development, data should be collected from all members of the team to determine how effectively it functions.

Some managers will want to skip data collection and start the planning and action phase. But it is important to collect data from the team members, because, instead of having one view—the manager's—there will be multiple views of how the team is functioning. This should result in a truer picture of the team's strengths and weaknesses. By contributing to the identification of problems to be addressed, team members' commitment to their resolution is increased.

There are occasions when in-depth data collection may not be necessary. If you are starting up a new team that has not worked together before, few data are available. The emphasis of a diagnosis with a new team should be upon what members need to know to function effectively as a team.

Temporary teams that have not previously met and will meet for only a very short period of time may prefer to merely poll the members to determine what concerns need to be addressed. However, for permanent or fairly long-term teams that have a work history, more extensive data collection is recommended. The two most common methods of determining the team's level of effectiveness are the interview and the questionnaire. My preference for managers doing their own team development is the questionnaire. It is easy to administer and maintains the anonymity of respondents during the early stages of team development. As team members realize that the process of team development is not punitive, and as their trust increases in how the data are to be used, this need for anonymity lessens. It is, however, a definite factor in the choice of techniques.

During an interview, respondents tend to become overexposed, saying things they may not wish to discuss in a team development meeting. Having an opportunity to think about what they say and write it down tends to reduce this, and they are more likely to be committed to talking about what they have written. Respondents also more readily recognize their comments from a questionnaire summary than from an interviewer's interpretation of what has been said.

If a consultant has been engaged, the consultant may choose to do interviews. Team members will have less need for anonymity with an external source, and the interview format provides opportunities for the consultant and team members to become better acquainted.

The manager should distribute the questionnaire to team members at a meeting and clearly state how the information will be used. Each participant, including the manager, should complete the questionnaire. Three to five days is a good time period for completion. A longer time provides opportunity for procrastination, and a shorter time does not allow for tight schedules.

Upon completion of the questionnaires, the participants should send them to a neutral source, a secretary or personnel department, for summarizing and compilation. The neutral source maintains some anonymity of response. The questionnaire content will be duplicated in a summary, but who said what will not be identified. Of course, with a small team it is often easy to identify who has made certain remarks. The manager, therefore, should make it clear to team members that anonymity will be maintained, but it is expected that team members will be willing to discuss what they have written on the questionnaire at a subsequent team meeting. Any comments that participants are unwilling to discuss should not be written on the questionnaire, because they are of no value to the team in discussion and problem solving of issues.

If the manager intends to collect the questionnaires and compile them himself, he should inform the team members so they understand that anonymity will not be protected. The summarization of the questionnaire results should be by frequency distribution for the areas where there is an opportunity to make a check mark. Comments made under each open-ended section should be typed verbatim on the summary sheet.

Summarizing Questionnaire Results

When the questionnaire results have been summarized, the manager should review them to determine the following:

1. Questionnaire results should contain no issues the manager does not wish to have discussed by the team. If they do, the manager should delete them from the data and explain why he has done so to the team members. Elimination of issues is seldom necessary. At this point, managers and team members have agreed they want to discuss how they can improve and are usually willing to discuss all issues identified.

2. The manager will want to establish what he believes are the priorities for the team to discuss. The team will be asked to identify its priorities at the first team meeting.

3. If the manager is working with a consultant, internal or external, there may be issues he will want to discuss with him prior to discussing them with the team members. Such discussions provide opportunities to clarify opinions and to express concerns, feelings, or constraints that could have negative impact on the team.

Team members should receive a summary of the questionnaire results one to two days before the first meeting. They should receive an Analysis of Key Issues form to determine what they believe are the priorities for the team development meeting. They should complete it and bring it with them to the meeting.

Manager's Review of Results with Team

Approximately three to four hours need to be allocated for the first meeting. It is not a good idea to conduct it in two parts, as it is the first time the team has met and there is a need to set priorities and begin discussing the problems. The manager should keep in mind that there is also a need for success at this first meeting. Therefore, enough time should be allocated so that the team completes its task of setting priorities, identifying subjects for discussion, and doing any prework needed for the next meeting.

To start the meeting, the manager should review the chronological events leading up to it. This may sound redundant. However, three or four weeks may have passed from the initial data collection until the questionnaire feedback meeting. Many things have happened within that time and team members may need a short review as to the purpose of the meeting and the events that have taken place so far. This review should cover:

Reasons for team development.
Sequence of events to date.
The purposes of the questionnaire feedback meeting.

These are the purposes of a feedback meeting:

1. To develop a mutual understanding of how the team is functioning. Participants should first try to understand what is being said in the questionnaire before debating it. Therefore, questions for understanding should be the first topic of discussion. It is important at this stage for the team to discuss what it does well, in addition to concerns, because the process of examining team effectiveness tends to zero in on areas for improvement. Discussing what the team does well identifies what should be continued and helps the members to feel good about the team's performance.

2. To set priorities. Priorities should be established to ensure that the team is working on the issues that are most important to members.

3. To decide whether to continue team development activities. The manager may want to reserve this decision for himself. However, at this point it is likely that the team will decide to continue. Involving team members in determining if and where the team needs to improve tremendously increases their commitment to improving team performance and their willingness to continue. Unless the data indicate that the team is functioning as effectively as possible, there will more than likely be issues that team members will want to improve.

4. To establish next steps. The outcomes of this first meeting should be an action plan that identifies priorities and a timetable for the next steps.

Meeting Guidelines

The manager should first give his interpretation of the questionnaire data and raise questions he wishes to have clarified. It is important to establish a climate of examination and open discussion regarding the team's functioning. The manager should proceed first, because team members are usually anxious to hear the manager's point of view. The manager's willingness to do this helps the other members enter into the discussions more openly. It establishes an atmosphere that says, "This will be an open discussion, I have a point of view. I want to hear yours."

To encourage the team members to talk, the manager should ask for their interpretations of the data and issues that they wish to have clarified. Each team member should have an opportunity to give his interpretation and ask questions.

When all questions have been clarified, each person should separately list his priority issues, and then publicly compile them to establish some general priorities. Keep in mind that participants will have already listed their priorities in filling out the Analysis of Key Issues form. However, they may change their minds upon hearing the discussion. It is not necessary at this point to establish a one through ten, specific priority list. However, establishing a major issue list is helpful so that everyone knows what the five or six most important ones are. It is important for teams to focus on the top priorities to avoid diluting efforts by trying to do everything and possibly accomplishing little.

The next step often involves setting a date for a future team meeting, to solve problems and develop action plans for the top priority issues. Prework assignments may also be established to ensure a productive meeting. Some teams decide to include this first meeting as part of a longer off-site meeting, usually two to three days. The team then would continue on with problem solving and action planning.

Characteristics of Data Feedback Meeting

The data feedback meeting is characterized by nervousness, laughing, and some joking. This may be the first time team members have discussed these subjects together, and it is normal to expect that a certain amount of tension and nervousness will exist. The tension usually dissipates as the team begins to discuss the issues and finds that the manager has established a climate that says, "It's okay to discuss these issues for the purpose of improving our performance."

An analogy between team development and how people go swimming can be helpful in understanding how teams proceed in this first and subsequent meetings. Some swimmers put on their bathing suits, run to the side of the pool, and immediately jump in without testing the water. Others, after putting on their suits, walk out to the pool, stick in a toe, and gradually immerse themselves, first their ankles, then their knees, until they are completely in the water. Teams move into team development in one of these two modes. Some jump in with both feet and begin to discuss the data readily, tackling the most difficult issues first. Other teams move in rather cautiously and want to test the water before they discuss the most difficult issues.

It is important that the manager's expectations of how rapidly the team will move not be too great. There is a fine line between continually moving the group along into more difficult and often more important issues and moving too rapidly with a team that is not ready to do so. There is usually a good reason that members are not willing to move rapidly, and it would be wise to look for these reasons and work with team members in overcoming any obstacles to freer conversation. The manager needs to occasionally remind the team members that they are moving rather cautiously into the water. They must then examine their process and choose to continue at that pace or move more rapidly.

The team may need to stop the problem solving and discuss its group process. Discussing the process allows the team to analyze why they are moving at the present rate of speed, if they should move faster, and, if so, what would help them to do that. A Group Process Guide, which will be discussed further in Chapter 6, can aid the team in examining and improving its work processes. Time should be allocated approximately every four hours, or more often if needed, during the data feedback and subsequent meetings for members to individually complete the form and then to discuss their responses for the purpose of improving the team's work processes.

The team is now ready to begin its action phase to improve its performance. The manager's next task is to do some planning to ensure that the subsequent team meetings are most productive. Chapter 5 outlines the items for consideration as the manager plans the team's first action meeting to work on the issues identified in the questionnaire.

TEAM DEVELOPMENT QUESTIONNAIRE

The following questions have been designed to *identify how* you feel *this team is functioning*, specifically, what *areas* you feel *need improvement.* The results will be compiled for discussion at an upcoming team development meeting. You will have an opportunity to review a summary of questionnaire results prior to the team meeting. You should be thinking about discussing your responses and others at this meeting.

Where there are multiple choices, check only one answer. Please be as candid and specific as possible.

Goals

1. List the goals that require members of this team to work together.

_____

_____

_____

_____

_____

2. With regard to the goals of this team, the people on this team are:

_____ Very committed.

_____ Somewhat committed.

_____ Somewhat resistant.

_____ Very resistant.

Team goals that I feel have *low* commitments are:

_____

_____

_____

Team goals that I feel have *high* commitments are:

_____

_____

_____

_____

3. To what extent do you know and understand each team member's goals?

_____ Very knowledgeable about team members' goals.

_____ Fairly knowledgeable about team members' goals.

_____ Somewhat vague knowledge of team members' goals.

_____ Very vague knowledge of team members' goals.

Goals I would like to know more about are:

_____

_____

_____

4. The goals of members of this team are:

_____ Strongly in conflict.

_____ Somewhat in conflict.

_____ A little in conflict.

_____ Not at all in conflict.

The key conflicts I see are:

_____

_____

_____

WORKING IN TEAMS

Roles

1. The roles of the members of the team are:

    _____ Very clear to me.

    _____ Fairly clear to me.

    _____ Somewhat unclear to me.

    _____ Very unclear to me.

    Areas I would like to have clarified concerning my role are:

    _____

    _____

    _____

    _____

    Areas in which I am unclear about what others expect of me are:

    _____

    _____

    _____

    Areas I would like to have clarified concerning others' roles are:

    _____

    _____

    _____

2. Team members' roles overlap:

    _____ Very much.

    _____ Quite a bit.

    _____ Somewhat.

    _____ Not at all.

Roles that overlap are:

_____

_____

3. Team members' roles that are in conflict are:

_____

_____

_____

Procedures

1. The decision-making process on matters that affect more than one member of the team is:

   _____ Very clear.

   _____ Fairly clear.

   _____ Somewhat unclear.

   _____ Very unclear.

   Decisions that need to be clarified are:

   _____

   _____

   _____

2. Thinking of all the communications within this team, I would say they are:

   _____ Good with all members of the team.

   _____ Good with some members of the team.

   _____ Good with very few members of the team.

   _____ Not very good with the majority of the team.

Please specify what subjects you feel need to be better communicated:

_____

_____

_____

3. Team meetings

____ Are very effective.

____ Are fairly effective.

____ Need some improvement.

____ Need much improvement.

Please specify how you would like team meetings to be improved:

_____

_____

_____

_____

4. I believe the leadership of this team

   a. Is helping the team's performance by:

_____

_____

_____

   b. Could improve the team's performance by:

_____

_____

_____

5. As teams work together, behavior patterns are established that help or hinder the team's performance such as:

> Following up or not following up on decisions.
> Raising or not raising sticky issues.
> Facilitating or delaying decisions.

Do you feel that there are such patterns that inhibit this team's effectiveness?

_____ Yes

_____ No

If yes, what are they?

_____

_____

_____

_____

Relationships

1. Conflicts within the team are:

_____ Openly discussed/resolved.

_____ Discussed somewhat.

_____ Very seldom mentioned.

_____ Not discussed at all.

A conflict that needs to be resolved to improve the team's performance is:

_____

_____

_____

2. Relationships I would like to discuss are:

_____

_____

_____

3. What is causing stress for you and/or other members of the team?

_____

_____

_____

Environmental Influences

1. What constraints or influences outside of the team keep it from working more effectively? Please explain.

_____

_____

_____

General

1. What do you believe are the team's key strengths?

_____

_____

_____

2. If you could, what would you do to make this team more effective?

_____

_____

_____

ANALYSIS OF KEY ISSUES

Please review the attached summary of responses to the team development questionnaire. Use this sheet to list what you believe are the major issues for discussion/resolution and indicate their relative priority. A = High, B = Medium, C = Low. These issues will provide the basis for discussion at an upcoming team development meeting.

1. Environmental Influences

_____

_____

_____

_____

2. Goals

_____

_____

_____

_____

3. Roles

_____

_____

_____

_____

4. Procedures

_____

_____

_____

_____

5. Relationships

_____

_____

_____

_____

6. Other

_____

_____

_____

_____

5

Planning Team Development Activities

On the basis of the issues identified by the team, the manager uses the materials in this section to plan action steps to improve the team's performance. Upon completing this section, the manager will have reviewed events to date to ensure that the team is ready to proceed and will have identified action steps to improve the team's performance. The following activities should require two to four hours:

- Manager reviews planning guide to ensure that team is ready to proceed to next steps.
- Manager plans next step and activities.
- Manager makes appropriate physical, logistical arrangements for next meeting.

Importance of Continual Planning

Planning is probably the most difficult task in team development, because it seldom involves interaction with other members of the team and is, therefore, often over-looked. However, planning is one of the more important parts of team development, because it determines whether the right activity is being undertaken at the appropriate time. Poor planning can undo much of the foundation that has been built to this point.

When the team has identified the priority issues for further work, the manager may begin to plan the activities the team should undertake to improve its performance. If the priority-setting meeting is combined with the problem-solving meeting in a two- to three-day sequence, the manager must do this planning before the priority-setting meeting. Obviously, he will not know the ultimate priority issues that will be identified. Most managers, however, sense these issues, or are able to identify several through an informal staff poll.

If the manager is working with a consultant, he and the consultant will serve as co-planners to work out the next steps. If he is not working with a consultant, he can do the planning on his own, or ask a team member to help think through the plans.

Planning is dynamic, not linear, and will take place at many stages during the team development process. To this point the manager has already done considerable planning about how he will do the diagnosis, conduct the feedback meeting, and so forth. The type of planning that takes place now is that of the specific action steps the team should undertake to improve its performance.

Planning Guide

In order to guide team activities, it is helpful to use the following checklist. *All items* should be considered before the first action meeting.

Phase I:

The first phase of planning involves a review of past activities and of the present status of team members as to their understanding and commitment.

_____ 1. Does everybody understand why they are involved in team development, what has taken place to date, and why the team is proceeding with the next steps?

_____ 2. If the manager is working with a consultant, are both their· roles clear?

_____ 3. Does the manager think he has enough valid information to proceed with the action steps? If not, he must collect additional information from the team or other sources before planning the next step.

_____ 4. Does the team have the power to resolve the issues identified? Inability to make any impact regarding issues identified can cause considerable frustration. If the issues can be resolved only by the manager or those working with power figures outside of the team, it may be necessary for the team to build its solidarity by first discussing issues within its control, in order that ultimately it may productively address environmental issues outside its immediate control. Plans for the resolution of environmental issues usually involve the team leader as the person who manages the team's interface with the outside.

_____ 5. Is the need for change clear? Do participants understand the payout and risk involved, and are they committed because they see the payout as worthwhile?

_____ 6. Are the members of the team, in the manager's estimation, willing to face the real problems and have a fruitful discussion? If not, further work must be done with individual members prior to discussion in a team setting.

Phase II:

The manager is now ready to plan specific activities for the team to address in the future. In planning these activities, the following conditions should be considered.

_____ 1. Plan an activity that all members are relatively comfortable with, that is, an activity that the culture can tolerate. If there are certain activities or training exercises that are inappropriate in the organization, the manager should select alternates that are accepted within the culture. The manager will have more knowledge than the external consultant in this regard and should provide the appropriate guidance.

_____ 2. Plan activities that keep the manager and the team members in their organizational roles. Some training exercises attempt to create equality among all members. However, the team and the manager know that the manager is still in charge at the end of the exercise and will have the final say regarding the direction of the team. If the activities planned for the team do not account for the differences in their roles, the activities will seem more like exercises and games, and less like solving real problems. Furthermore, the team will have difficulty transferring the behavior from the exercise into daily action.

If the manager is using an external consultant, it is also necessary that he not usurp the manager's role. The manager's role is to see that decisions are reached and that follow-up takes place. The consultant's role is to help with the team process and to explain whatever tasks the team is undertaking if the consultant has had experience with them and the manager has not.

_____ 3. Plan an activity that will give you quick success. Do not plan an activity that will take six months to complete as the first team undertaking.

_____ 4. Make sure the goal of the activity being undertaken is clear to all members of the team. A good clue that it is not will be continual questions during the activity, such as "Why are we doing this?" or "What is this about?" or "What are we supposed to be doing?" or "What is it we are trying to accomplish?" At times this may also be a smoke screen for the members who do not want to proceed. The manager must stop and check out exactly what people are trying to say. Are they unclear about the activity or are they trying to slow it down or stop it?

_____ 5. Plan activities that are problem-oriented as well as training-oriented. It is necessary that the group work on a real issue and not entirely on training exercises. The more the group solves real problems rather than training exercises, the better members are able to transfer the learnings to their jobs and the more productive they will feel the activity has been. There may be some sacrifice in learning about how to solve future problems by focusing on real issues, because the team members may become preoccupied with the problem and pay little attention to how they are working on it. It is often necessary after an issue has been resolved to roll the cameras back and ask the group to examine its process; how members worked on the issue to determine if these are processes they can apply in the future.

Phase III:

In addition to ascertaining that the team is ready for team development and planning specific activities, the manager must make plans for the physical setting and the length of the actual meetings. These plans will vary, depending upon time and cost constraints.

_____ 1. Initial meetings should take place at a neutral location. Because these meetings often entail covering subjects that team members do not regularly discuss, they should not be in the office of the boss or a team member. It is preferable to find a conference room away from phones and interruptions. It may even be desirable to hold the meetings away from the office. However, this may give the impression that team development is something you do when you go away from the office, and not something you do on a daily basis at work locations.

___ 2. The room should be well ventilated and well lighted. Comfortable chairs that can be moved about to form different subgroups are preferable. If a large number of materials are needed, a table to put them on can be provided. However, the presence of a table in a room provides more structure and a possible obstacle to free-flowing discussion. When members can sit in a circle and see one another without the obstruction of a table and without the status positions represented by the two ends of the table, there is usually much freer discussion. The absence of a table indicates that this meeting will be different from those experienced in the past and helps to set the climate that participants are to work in a different mode than in the past. Staffs cannot meet at all times without tables, as they will need them for materials. However, these first few meetings are important in establishing an open climate and in encouraging free-flowing communications.

___ 3. Provide adequate materials; a flip chart, magic markers, and masking tape will allow the manager to record participants' ideas visibly and to hang them around the room for reference throughout the meeting. Each team member should have copies of whatever materials are to be used during the program and be aware of the timetable and schedule of the meetings so that their travel plans can be made accordingly.

___ 4. Consider the team members' schedules when planning the length of meetings. Some teams like to undertake activities once a week for four hours. Other teams like to meet away from the workplace for one, two, or three days and undertake a number of activities. There are, of course, advantages and disadvantages to both approaches. The advantage of undertaking activities once a week is that prework can be done and follow-up can take place between activities. Undertaken in this manner, it appears to be the ongoing responsibility of the team rather than extra work. This approach may not be appropriate for some teams that cannot meet four hours every week. Some teams find it more convenient to meet for one, two, or three days, covering a number of subjects, and to make follow-up assignments for a subsequent meeting. An extended period of time allows teams to accomplish more within a shorter time frame and to delve into subjects in more depth if needed. Meeting for short periods of time for a team that is having difficulty getting into the subject may never allow enough time for members to really engage and resolve issues.

After reviewing the planning guide and ensuring that all points have been covered to his satisfaction, the manager is ready to implement a number of actions that are designed to help the team improve its performance. Chapter 6 contains these action tools and instructions for using them.

Selecting Appropriate Tasks

The guide, Selecting Appropriate Tasks, will help the manager and the team to determine which tasks will improve their performance on the basis of the diagnosis. It contains a short description of each of the action steps, what issues they are designed to address, and the approximate amount of time required to undertake them. Activities appear in the recommended sequence for use, starting with those designed to work on goal issues and ending with environmental influences.

A complete team development program includes one or more action steps to address issues in each of the major categories in the team development hierarchy. However, it is not likely that the team would undertake all the activities listed. It is more likely it will undertake one within each major category. The activities are designed as a cafeteria approach so that teams can select those that are most appropriate.

SELECTING APPROPRIATE TASKS

When a team has identified issues for resolution, it is necessary to plan action steps to resolve them. The following is a guide to help you select the appropriate action steps.

Issue	*Tasks*
Goals	1. Identifying team mission helps identify and clarify the team's purpose.
	2. Team goals helps identify and clarify goals that require coordination by two or more members of the team. Teams also discuss how members should be rewarded for team goals.
	3. Sharing individual and team goals helps identify and resolve any goal or resource conflicts.
Roles	4. Job/responsibilities defines team members' responsibilities and increases understanding of roles. It is particularly helpful for new as well as existing teams.
	5. Role mapping is designed to identify team members' interdependencies, expectations of one another, influence and communications patterns, and role overlaps, or conflicts.
Work Process	6. Team decision making provides criteria for identifying the major team decisions.
	7. Team meetings guide identifies subjects for meetings and how each should be handled and provides a format for meeting agendas.
	8. Communications helps to identify what needs to be better communicated, the frequency needed, how, and by whom.
	9. Group process guide helps the team continually examine how well the members are working together. It also keeps the team in the role of

process observer and lessens the team's dependency on the manager or a third party to fulfill that role.

Relationships 10. <u>Resolving differences</u> provides a format and guidelines for two or more members of the team to resolve differences or conflicts.

11. <u>Resolving relationship issues</u> is designed for the team whose members are experiencing a strain in relationships. It deals with problems that occur as a consequence of people working together on a regular basis. It is not as extensive as task 10, which deals with full-blown conflicts.

SELECTING APPROPRIATE TASKS

Issue Addressed	Tasks	Approximate Time Required
Goals	1. Identifying team mission	1–4 hours
	2. Team goals	2–4 hours
	3. Sharing individual and team goals	3–4 hours
Roles	4. Job/responsibilities	3–4 hours
	5. Role mapping	4 hours
Work Process	6. Team decision making	2–4 hours
	7. Team meetings	2–4 hours
	8. Communications	2–4 hours
	9. Group process guide	2–4 hours
Relationships	10. Relationship/Conflict Model	2–4 hours
	11. Resolving relationship issues	2–4 hours

6

Implementing
Team Improvement
Activities

This chapter discusses the tasks the team would undertake to improve its performance. A complete team development program would include all the action steps outlined. However, most teams would not need to use all the actions but would select those that the diagnosis indicated as needed. A typical sequence of team development activities might be:

- The team meets to discuss and resolve any issues relating to goals. Requires three to four hours.
- The team meets to clarify roles and resolve conflicts between the roles of members. Requires four hours.
- The team meets to discuss how it can improve communications and team meetings. Requires two to four hours.
- Team members meet to discuss how they can improve working relationships. Requires three to four hours.
- The team meets to plan how to approach and resolve issues with other groups, the organization, or other

outside influences. Action materials will depend on the issue. Open systems planning as described by Beckhard is a useful tool for environmental issues. Requires two to four hours.

Time requirements are based on a team of six. Larger teams require more time.

Starting Point

There are many tasks that teams can undertake to improve their performance. Well-functioning teams undertake self-improvement tasks as part of their regular work routine. From the activities described in this chapter, the manager should select action steps that will best meet the team's needs. He may also wish to involve the team in this selection.

The typical starting point is with a goal improvement activity, then roles, procedures, and relationships. Having done this, teams are usually ready to tackle the outside world or environmental influences. There are times when the environmental influences seem so intertwined with other issues, such as goals and roles, that it is impossible to treat them separately. If the manager finds that the team's energy is so focused on one area that progress will not be made until it is resolved, he may wish to start with roles, procedures, or relationships.

Occasionally, relationship problems between team members need to be resolved before there can be productive resolution of other issues. Sometimes the problem-solving and meeting skills of the team need some work before it can productively tackle its goals.

At whatever point the team starts, the following tasks are designed to help teams resolve the types of issues most frequently confronting them.

Identifying Team Mission

The team's mission determines its direction and goals. Teams operate effectively to the extent the mission is clear and agreed upon. After agreeing on a mission, the team can then identify and reach agreement on its goals.

Each team member, including the team leader, should write his statement of the team's mission or basic reason for being. The team should then discuss each statement and agree on a team mission. The team mission should be written, rather than spoken, to avoid misunderstandings or confusion. The team's mission is its overall reason for being, what the team was created to do. For example, the team's mission might be:

To maximize profit.
To provide a service to line managers.
To implement Project X.

This team's mission is_____

_____

_____

_____

_____

_____

_____

_____

The agreed-upon mission should provide a focus for the team to determine its goals, strategies, and actions. If it does not, it may be written too broadly.

Team Goals

Team goals are those that

1. Require the coordination, at a minimum, of two or more members of the team to accomplish; that cannot be accomplished by individuals, but require a team.
2. Are critical to the success or failure of the overall team mission and whose outcomes can be influenced by two or more of its members.
3. Are the product of the accomplishment of several individual members' goals, with each person's contribution depending upon or influencing the other.
4. Members believe they can influence and help accomplish.

TEAM GOALS

I. Using those criteria, list what you believe to be team goals:

A. Goal _____

   Coordination/resource required _____

   _____

   Team member(s) _____

   _____

B. Goal _____

   Coordination/resource required _____

   _____

   Team member(s) _____

   _____

C. Goal _____

   Coordination/resource required _____

   _____

   Team member(s) _____

   _____

D. Goal _____

   Coordination/resource required _____

   _____

   Team member(s) _____

   _____

II. The team may choose to rewrite existing individual goals as team goals or write new ones. If so, how should they be written? What responsibility will each member have?

A. New Goal _____

Responsibility _____

_____

B. New Goal _____

Responsibility _____

_____

C. New Goal _____

Responsibility _____

_____

D. New Goal _____

Responsibility _____

_____

III. Team members should discuss whether they are to be rewarded as a team or individually for the accomplishment of team goals.

Will rewards be based on team accomplishment or on individual accomplishment?

Who will determine the level of accomplishment: the manager, the team, or other?

What criteria or benchmarks will be used to determine the extent of goal accomplishment?

How will members be rewarded?

1. Percent of reward based on accomplishment of individual goals?
2. Percent of reward based on accomplishment of team goals?
3. Other?

SHARING INDIVIDUAL AND TEAM GOALS

Teams exist because individuals are working together to accomplish a common goal, with each member of the team performing various functions. The following process is designed to share individual goals and identify or clarify team goals. Each member of the team will write his responses for each section and will be asked to discuss them at a future team meeting. The purpose of the meeting will be to gain understanding and agreement on individual and team goals.

1. Briefly list your major goals for the year, for review with the team.

   _____

   _____

   _____

   _____

   _____

2. Which of these goals requires coordination or working with one or more other members of the team, or the use of resources from another's area? List the objective, the coordination or resource required, and the other team members.

   A. Goal _____

      Coordination/resource required _____

      _____

      Team member(s) _____

      _____

   B. Goal _____

      Coordination/resource required _____

      _____

Team member(s) _____

_____

C. Goal _____

Coordination/resource required _____

_____

Team member(s) _____

_____

D. Goal _____

Coordination/resource required _____

_____

Team member(s) _____

_____

3. Upon reviewing your goals and the coordination required, do you fore-see limited resource or coordination problems for which the team needs to plan? Please describe.

_____

_____

_____

4. Are there conflicting goals on this team? If so, what are they? What do you recommend?

A. Goal Conflict _____

_____

Recommendation _____

_____

B. Goal Conflict _____

_____

Recommendation _____

_____

C. Goal Conflict _____

_____

Recommendation _____

_____

D. Goal Conflict _____

_____

Recommendation _____

_____

5. Do you believe that goals need to be changed (clarified, made more specific, or written as shared goals)? Please explain.

_____

_____

_____

_____

6. Do you have other comments or suggestions regarding goals? Please specify.

_____

_____

_____

_____

JOB/RESPONSIBILITIES

Job/responsibilities is a task that helps each member of the team prepare a description of his job. Its purpose is to increase the team members' understanding of others' responsibilities and to clarify each team member's role. It is helpful to existing and newly formed teams to give each member an understanding of the responsibilities of others.

   Prior to a meeting scheduled to discuss responsibilities, each team member should complete responses for the following and come prepared to discuss them.

A. Major pieces of work for which you are responsible.

Work _____

Responsibility _____

Work _____

Responsibility _____

Work _____

Responsibility _____

Work _____

Responsibility _____

B. Pieces of work in which you are unclear about your or others' responsibility. Specify what needs clarification.

_____

_____

_____

_____

_____

C. Work that needs to be coordinated with other members of the team. (Specify team members.)

Work _____

Coordination required _____

_____

Team member(s) _____

_____

Work _____

Coordination required _____

_____

Team member(s) _____

_____

Work _____

Coordination required _____

_____

Team member(s) _____

_____

Work _____

Coordination required _____

_____

Team member(s) _____

_____

D. Responsibilities that you believe are not being addressed or are falling through the cracks.

_____

_____

_____

E. Areas of your job where you believe your responsibilities overlap or conflict with those of other members of the team.

_____

_____

_____

_____

Team Discussion

Each person should review his responsibilities and identify what he wishes to discuss further or change about them. Team members should cover the following questions in reviewing their responsibilities:

1. Are there conflicts between your responsibilities and those of others?
2. Are their differences between how you see your responsibilities on this team and how others see them?

The team should discuss and reach agreement on each person's review of responsibilities and identify needed action steps. The following questions should be discussed after all members have reviewed their responsibilities.

3. Is there overlapping of team members' responsibilities? How should these overlaps be handled?
4. What actions are indicated to clarify roles or improve how this team functions?

Role Mapping

The roles we play are determined by our position in the organizational hierarchy, our functional and job responsibilities, and, to a great extent, by expectations. The purpose of role mapping is to review how team members interact and what they expect of each other. It should result in individual or group actions to change or clarify roles, expectations, and how team members interact. Each team member should draw a map depicting his role and explain it to the team.

Drawing Map

A. Each member of the team should individually draw a role map (on 26″ × 32″ flip chart paper, if available). The map should contain the names of the team members and possibly those of people outside the team who have a significant impact on your performance in the team. The time allotted for this activity is 45 minutes.

1. Draw circles of different sizes to represent the relative influence you feel the person has on decisions that have impact on the team. The larger the circle, the greater the influence.
2. Arrange distance between circles to represent the perceived amount of interdependence between you and others. The closer the circles to yours, the more interdependent you are with them.
3. Show lines with arrows of varying width to represent direction and amount of communication between you and others. (See Figure 4.)
4. On a separate page prepare a brief commentary or listing of the 3 to 5 major things each of the other team members expect of you.
5. Prepare a brief listing of what you expect of them.

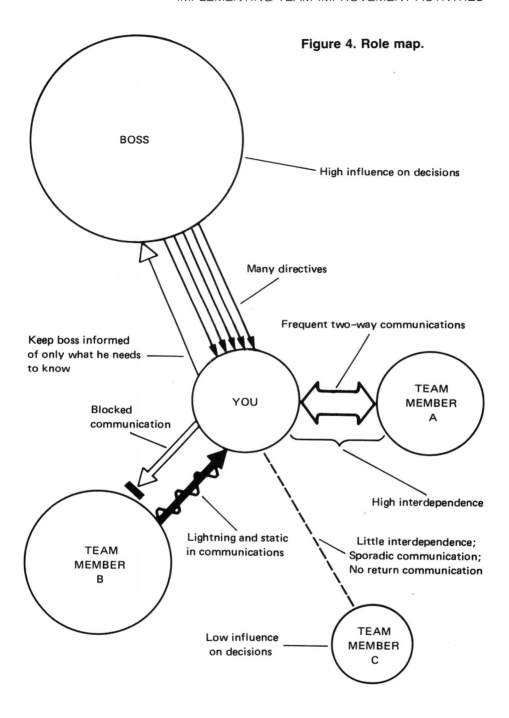

Figure 4. Role map.

6. Review your map and identify what you want to change or discuss regarding your role, or those of others. The following questions may be helpful in this review.

   a. Do you want to change:

      Your communications with members of the team?

      The amount of influence you have?

      The extent of interdependence with others?

   b. Are the expectations that others have of you, as you perceive them, and that you have of them the right expectations for optimal team performance? If not, how would you change them?

   c. Is this the best role for you and for the team's overall effectiveness? If not, how should your role be changed?

Discussing Maps

Each person should explain his map and answer the preceding questions. The time limit should be approximately 30–45 minutes per map. Team members may ask questions for understanding but should hold items for discussion until the person has completed his explanation. Discussion of issues or concerns that should be resolved by only a few members of the team should be noted on a chalkboard or flip chart and scheduled for a later time. Some subjects can be discussed and resolved immediately; others may take considerable time and should be held either until all members have reviewed their maps or at a later date. Be sure to note on a chalkboard for future reference any discussions that are to be held later.

When all maps have been explained and discussed, the total group should review and discuss the following questions. Members should individually review the questions (10 minutes), make notes, and then discuss them as a group.

1. Do team members' roles overlap? How should the overlaps be handled?
2. Are team members' roles in conflict?
3. Are there differences between my expectations and the expectations of others?
4. What actions are indicated to improve how we function as a team?

Team Decision Making

In order for teams to effectively make decisions, they must first identify which decisions they should make as a team and which should be made by individuals, and how each member of the team should participate. The following activity is designed to help teams decide which decisions they will work on as a team by giving the team some criteria to determine what constitutes a team decision. Some examples of what other teams have identified as team decisions are policy, resource allocation, strategy, goal establishment, and major changes in organization. A team decision is usually made by consensus. All members discuss the decision until there is general agreement. It may not be possible to reach total agreement, but all parties should at least be willing to try to put the decision into effect.

Identifying Team Decisions

Individually list the three or more decisions that you believe should be made by the team as contrasted to decisions that would be made by individuals. These should be decisions that occur on a regular or frequent basis, not a once-only type of decision. Then review the criteria in the following chart for a team decision to determine how many of these criteria the decision fits. The total team should then discuss their answers to determine which are consensus decisions. For example, if a decision fits criterion A, it is more likely that the decision should be made as a team than if it fits only criterion B. Criterion D by itself is probably not a sufficient reason for a team decision.

Even though decisions should be made by the team, that does not mean all members have a vote. The manager or a member of the team may reserve the right to the final decision after consulting with all or some part of the team, depending on the subject and who has knowledge of or is affected by the decision. Such a decision would fall into category E. The team should identify who is to be consulted prior to the decision or informed of the final result. It is likely that each team member will have a fair number of decisions that fall into category E. If there is some doubt as to whether a decision fits into this category, it should be reviewed with the team to determine how it should best be made.

The criteria for team decisions are:

1. The knowledge needed to make the decision is distributed across several members of the team and the quality of the decision will be greatly improved by involving them.
2. Several members of the team will need to implement the decision and therefore need to understand and agree with it.
3. The decision will have impact on the work areas of several members of the team.
4. There is enough time for a team discussion and decision.

A decision is *individual* when it lies within one person's responsibility who basically has the knowledge needed to make it. However, prior to making the decision, he may want to consult with others to acquire additional information or advice. He may also want to inform others of his decision prior to implementation.

IDENTIFYING TEAM DECISIONS

INSTRUCTIONS:

1. List the decisions to be made.
2. Identify which criteria apply.
3. Determine whether it should be a team or individual decision.
4. Determine when the decisions will be made and who will be involved.

Decision	TEAM (see scale below)	INDIVIDUAL Decision within one person's area of responsibility; he has the information. List team members to be:
1.		Consulted
		Informed
2.		Consulted
		Informed
3.		Consulted
		Informed
4.		Consulted
		Informed

SCALE FOR EVALUATING TEAM DECISION

A Knowledge distributed across team, quality improved by involving team.
B Members will implement, need to understand and agree.
C Decision will have impact on the work areas of several members.
D There is enough time for a team discussion and decision.

When will these decisions be made and *which team members* will be involved?

1. _____

_____

2. _____

_____

3. _____

_____

4. _____

_____

Team Meetings

Meetings often continue longer than everyone would like because the leader and the participants have not identified in advance whether a meeting is really needed, what subjects should be covered, and what they wish to accomplish. Some groups discuss for hours subjects that do not require a decision. Either the decision had already been made or it was not the group's responsibility or province to make it. In these instances, the decision maker is really only informing the group to keep them updated of his actions.

Making the best use of meetings requires that you are discussing the right subjects and using the appropriate process. The team meetings guide is designed to help identify subjects the team should cover during a meeting and how they should be handled. Each person should complete this form prior to a team meeting so as to discuss how to improve meetings. At the meeting each person should explain his list. Although the initial classification of how a subject is to be dealt with is the responsibility of the initiator of the subject, it is necessary to get the group's concurrence to the classification. A flip chart to summarize points or copies of all lists would be helpful. The team should agree on a final list as an agenda for future meetings.

TEAM MEETINGS

Subjects for Team Meetings	Person Responsible or Initiator	Action Required (see scale below)	Time Allocated
1.			
2.			
3.			
4.			
5.			

Scale for Indicating Action

1 *Information* Subject presented for information only. No decision is needed and little discussion required.
2 *Consultative* Initiator of subject wants the group's ideas and feedback. The discussion or action is the responsibility of the initiator.
3 *Planning/Discussion* Initiator presents an issue often with no predetermined decision. The group collectively plans and discusses next steps. The final decision is the responsibility of the initiator.
4 *Consensus* Decision is made by the group. Consensus is reached when all members can "live with" the decision.
5 *Unanimous* The decision is made when all members agree.

Communications: What, How, Who

Communications can frequently be improved by identifying what needs to be better communicated, how, by whom, and to whom. The *communications* guide is designed for this purpose. Please complete the following form for each member of the team, identifying subjects you think they need to better communicate for you to most effectively do your job. Each person receiving a message should respond to the sender's proposal for improving communications by completing the bottom part of this form. It is quite likely that persons may receive the same message from several team members. Individuals should identify who they need to meet with and the subject for further discussion by completing the summary which should then be the basis for identifying who needs to meet to discuss how they can improve communications. It is likely that members may need to meet in pairs or trios to discuss how to improve.

COMMUNICATIONS GUIDE

Message to _____ Message from _____

Subjects for Better Communications	Preferred Method	Fre-quency	What I Am Willing to Do to Improve Communications

Receiver's Response to Message Sender:

A. I agree with your proposal and will implement it.

B. We need to discuss your proposal, and I have the following ideas to improve our communications.

_____

_____

_____

SUMMARY OF COMMUNICATIONS MESSAGES

Subjects for Better Communications	People Involved	Actions Taken

Group Process Guide

Periodically, at the end of team meetings, 15 minutes should be set aside for each member of the team to complete this form; the team should discuss the results and make any needed changes in how the team is functioning. This periodic, ongoing critique of your team's performance is necessary for the maintenance and improvement of team performance.

After each person has individually completed the form, discuss your answers as a group and document any needed changes or follow-up actions agreed upon. To receive the most value from your discussions they should focus on areas where there is a discrepancy of response or where members think there should be improvement.

For each subject please indicate your rating and be prepared to discuss your reasons for it.

GROUP PROCESS GUIDE

1 = Minimal teamwork conditions   5 = Ideal teamwork conditions

1. *Communications*
   How effectively do members of the team communicate to each other?

   Very little and/or   Members communicate
   ineffective   openly and
   communication.   effectively.

   |_____|_____|_____|_____|_____|
        1   2   3   4   5

2. *Involvement/Participation*

Discussion is
dominated by
a few members.

All members are
involved and
participate freely.

| 1 | 2 | 3 | 4 | 5 |

3. *Decision Making*

Decisions are delayed,
made without involvement
of those with valid information, have low acceptance.

Decisions are timely,
involve those with
relevant information,
have high acceptance.

| 1 | 2 | 3 | 4 | 5 |

4. *Meetings/Subjects*

Meetings are
ineffective, do not
cover relevant topics.

Meetings are effective
and cover
relevant topics.

| 1 | 2 | 3 | 4 | 5 |

5. *Attitudes Toward Differences Within Group*

Members avoid
differences,
smooth them over.

Members respect and
accept differences
and work them through.

| 1 | 2 | 3 | 4 | 5 |

6. The team is doing the following well: _____

_____

_____

_____

_____

_____

7. Other factors influencing the team's effectiveness are: _____

_____

_____

_____

_____

_____

Relationship/Conflict Model

Relationship problems among team members are often symptomatic of problems rooted in disagreements over goals, roles, procedures, or environmental factors. Their resolution lies in solving the root cause rather than treating the relationship. If, however, the conflict is the result of a values difference or a personality clash, or the relationship is so strained that team members cannot work on the root cause, it may be necessary to approach the problem by working directly on the relationship.

The following model encourages an open discussion of the problem, identifies differences, builds understanding of each point of view, reduces defensiveness, and begins a mutual problem-solving approach to resolving the conflict.

As the manager of two team members who have a relationship problem, you must check to see that three general conditions exist before the two parties meet. If one or more of these conditions are not met, you must do some prework to establish them.

General Conditions for Conflict Resolution

1. *The two parties are interdependent.* The interdependence is usually the basis for a conflict and is also necessary to gain resolution. If the two members need each other to do their jobs, they have a basis for resolving the conflict. It is a paradox that this interdependence is usually also the cause of the conflict.

2. *There is something in it for both parties.* The conflict is not likely to be resolved unless something is to be gained by each of the team members involved. If a member sees nothing to be gained, or if he already is getting all he wants, there will be little incentive to resolve the conflict.

3. *Both members have some power in the situation.* Both members should have the ability to reward or sanction the other and should not feel that the other is all-powerful or that he is powerless as they enter into the conflict resolution meeting.

Criteria for Productive Conflict Resolution

If your check indicates that the general conditions for conflict resolution exist, you are then ready to enter into the problem-solving process. In order for this meeting to be most productive, the following criteria must be met.

1. There must be a mutual definition and understanding of the problem on the part of both parties.

2. Both parties must be willing to admit that they may be a part of the problem.

3. Both parties must have an opportunity to ventilate or blame the other. This is a necessary catharsis before people can calmly discuss and resolve problems.

4. There must be some binding quality to the agreements reached. Both parties need to feel that they have sanctions if the other member does not live up to his part of the agreement.

5. Both parties must receive something from the conflict resolution. There must be a *quid pro quo*. If not, both parties will feel they have received nothing and will not honor the agreements.

6. Both parties, with the help of a third party, usually the manager, must exhibit the following behaviors:
   a. Good listening.
   b. Low defensiveness.
   c. The ability to stay in a problem-solving mode.

Manager's Role as Third Party

It is necessary that both parties agree there is a relationship problem or conflict and they wish to resolve it. It is your role as the manager to discuss this with both parties to ensure they are willing to proceed. Once you have determined they are willing to meet and resolve the conflict, you will ask each party to respond to the following questions. They will be asked to bring their written responses with them to a future meeting at which they will be asked to discuss their responses with one another.

1. What is the problem as you perceive it?

2. What does the other person do that contributes to the problem? Be specific about how he affects your ability to do your job effectively.

3. What do you do that contributes to the problem?

4. What do you want/need from the other person so as to effectively perform your job?

The first meeting should be at a neutral place where both parties feel they can speak freely without being interrupted or overheard. Approximately two hours should be scheduled for this meeting. The manager's role is to serve as a traffic cop to ensure that due process takes place and both parties' points of view are given consideration. You are not to act as a judge to decide which party to the conflict is right or wrong. Rather, you should be seen as neutral by both parties, having no vested interest in one party winning over the other. If you perceive that you have a vested interest, another member of the team or an internal or external consultant should serve as the third party.

At the meeting you will first ask participant A to give his answers to questions 1 through 4. As he is doing this, participant B must listen but not interrupt. If B has questions, he should jot them down but continue to listen to what A has to say. When A has finished reviewing questions 1 through 4, B can ask questions for understanding but not for debate. Participant B then should respond with his answers to questions 1 through 4 while A listens. When B has finished, A can ask questions for understanding. At this point some discussion and debate is helpful. After both parties have had an opportunity to clearly express their points of view, both parties should respond to question 5, which is:

5. What first step can you take to resolve the problem?

Note: You are asking each person to identify what he can do, not what he wants the other to do to resolve the problem. Both parties should read their responses to question 5, after which problem solving should take place to reach a mutually satisfactory solution.

By reviewing the criteria for productive conflict resolution, one can see how the model incorporates them into the problem-solving process. Step 1 of the model results in a mutual definition of the problem. Step 2 provides an opportunity for both parties to blame the other and to vent their feelings about the situation. Question 3 provides an opportunity for both parties to be introspective and to admit that they contribute as well to the problem. Question 4 examines the interdependence between the two parties—what it is they want and need from one another to effectively perform their jobs. It also examines the *quid pro quo*—what both might get from the resolution of the conflict. Question 5 identifies what each party is willing to do or give to resolve the conflict. Question 5 also moves both parties into a problem-solving mode. The third party assures that good listening takes place and that both parties stay in as low a defensive posture as possible. The discussion should continue until both parties feel that a mutually satisfactory resolution has been reached.

Resolving Relationship Issues

Relationships become strained as a matter of course as people who are interdependent work together. Sometimes they improve by doing nothing. More often they get worse if nothing is done and the interdependence and reason for dispute remain. Team members who learn how to address and resolve these issues can maintain a productive relationship as well as a high level of team effectiveness.

As you think of your relationship with other members of the team, identify any issues you would like to discuss by completing questions 1 through 3. You will then notify the other person that you have an issue you would like to discuss and you give him a copy of your responses to review. He should then complete questions 1 through 3 and give you a copy to review. You should both meet at a mutually determined time to discuss your responses and reach a resolution.

ANALYSIS OF RELATIONSHIPS

1. A relationship issue I have as we work together is (Be specific; describe what the other person does that keeps you from being most effective.)

2. What I am willing to do to help resolve the problem is

3. What I would like you to do to help resolve the problem is

Environmental Influence

Environmental issues can be myriad, as are the appropriate actions. The team must determine in each case what is appropriate and who should implement each action. The action often requires the team leader to interact with individuals outside of the team. This need for interaction was experienced by a plant manager and his team. They were experiencing considerable internal conflict as well as performance problems. They hired 300 extra people one week and had to lay them off the next. They ran out of raw materials and suddenly the next week had six extra boxcars of raw materials. The plant manager believed the problems resulted from poor teamwork. Upon first hearing, the problem seemed to be one of coordination and communications. However, the diagnosis revealed that the problem lay with the interfaces between the team and the larger organization.

The corporate marketing department had neglected to tell the team that it had postponed the national introduction of a product so the plant did not need the 300 extra people. Sales forgot to tell the plant that the test market would start earlier and end earlier than originally planned, which accounted for the shortage and over-ordering of raw materials.

These problems required that the team members and the leader manage the interface with the corporate departments. Eventually, a three-way meeting was set up involving manufacturing, sales, and marketing to resolve the issue.

In this case the job responsibilities and communications tasks were helpful in resolving the problem. However, each environmental issue has to be carefully examined to determine the appropriate resolution.

7

Evaluation and Follow-up

To determine how well the team has done and what else may be needed, evaluation is necessary. The team will be asked at the beginning of its team development activities to complete a questionnaire evaluating the team's performance. Upon completion of the team improvement activities, the team will evaluate how much it has improved and what follow-up is needed. The sequence is as follows:

- Manager and team complete evaluation prior to and at the conclusion of the team development effort. See the Analyzing Team Effectiveness Form later in this chapter.
- Results are summarized.
- Manager reviews results and plans meeting to review with team. Time required is one hour.
- Results are sent to team members for review.
- Team meets to discuss results and determine if any additional work is needed. Allot two hours.
- Team evaluates its progress periodically, at least once

a month, at team meetings through use of verbal critique or rating scale, and determines any needed changes in team's functioning. See the Group Process Guide in Chapter 6.

The primary criterion for evaluating team development efforts is whether or not the team functions effectively. Is the team accomplishing its tasks? Is the process the team uses being improved? Is the result of team development a more effectively functioning team with less stress, greater member satisfaction, and greater personal growth of its members?

In addition to determining if the team has improved, evaluation determines what else needs to be improved. It is this second purpose that teams frequently find most valuable.

Evaluation should take place at several stages in the team development effort. Formal evaluations should take place at the beginning and at the completion of a team development effort. Evaluation should also take place after every team development meeting as a monitoring device to determine how well the team is doing.

The team should not be alarmed if the evaluation after a few activities shows that the team's performance either has not improved or perhaps has decreased. This happens when teams engage in improvement activities and become aware of how much more they have yet to improve. As a result, they set their standards higher. Therefore, they view their present performance as being less satisfactory because of those higher expectations.

Evaluation Tools

Two tools—the Analyzing Team Effectiveness Form and the Group Process Guide—are available for evaluation. The first is used as a beginning-and-end evaluation of the team's effectiveness. To get a before-and-after measure, team members complete the Analyzing Team Effectiveness Form at the beginning of the team development effort and again at the end. The second tool can be used at any point during the team development effort to determine how well the team's process is progressing.

The team could also use the original team development questionnaire as a before-and-after measurement. The team's performance can also be evaluated by establishing improvement objectives at the beginning of the team development effort and measuring the extent of achievement of those objectives.

The team manager can ask his supervisor to identify improvement targets for the team development effort, and the evaluation can ascertain how well the team has met those targets.

Interviewing members of the team is another way of determining whether or not they believe the team has improved its performance. The team members' evaluation or feelings about their own effectiveness, although not a rigorous scientific methodology, can be an important source of information to determine what else the team needs to do to improve. If it is a service-oriented organization, such as personnel, the areas that it works with will have an opinion as to whether or not its interaction with them has improved. If it is a team that needs to interact with other parts of the organization, those sections or departments will have an opinion as to whether or not the team's performance has changed. The subordinates of the team members may also have perceptions about changes in the team's performance.

Dilemmas of Evaluation

The closer the team is to major units of productivity or output as measured by the organization, the easier it is to evaluate the effect of team development. For example, it is easy to evaluate if an athletic team is performing well or not; it will have more points or a better win-loss record than the other team. It is easy to evaluate if a production team is performing well, because production units can be measured.

In service organizations, where the output tends to be decisions rather than units of production, it becomes more difficult to measure the team's output. It is more difficult to measure whether service organizations are providing better service or making better decisions than in product organizations that have the capability of measuring units of productivity.

Measurement also becomes more difficult as you move up the hierarchy. For example, in working with the president of a firm and his staff, the marketing manager informed the production and research managers that because of the way they had set goals for the year he had lost $1 million on his marketing plan. As a result of that discussion, they agreed to set goals in a different manner. However, there was no way of measuring whether or not that specific action in the future would save the organization $1 million.

Evaluation may sometimes be needed to justify team development efforts to higher levels of management. Whatever the reason, teams should address the questions of evaluation at the beginning of the team development effort:

What do we want to improve?
What kind of evaluation data do we need?
How will we collect data and how often?
What will we do with the evaluation results?

The following form, Analyzing Team Effectiveness, is designed as a before-and-after measurement of team members' perceptions of how well the team is functioning.

Analyzing Team Effectiveness

This form is designed to stimulate an analysis and discussion of how well your team is functioning. Upon completion of the form by each team member, the team should meet to discuss the ratings. It will be the responsibility of the team leader and the team to analyze and evaluate its performance and take whatever steps are needed for improvement.

Two factors represented in this form determine a team's effectiveness. Section I analyzes what tasks the team is accomplishing, if goals are being achieved, and how well deadlines are being met. Section II analyzes the team's process, how decisions are made, how communications are handled, and the planning process.

The importance or relative weight given to these two items, task and process, and to each factor (planning, goals, listening) in determining the team's composite rating is to be determined by the team itself, keeping in mind that the process used determines the end result. Additionally, if the process is good but the task is not accomplished, the team has not been ultimately effective. Therefore, it is a blending of these two factors that determines the team's effectiveness.

ANALYZING TEAM EFFECTIVENESS FORM

For each subject, please indicate your rating and briefly state your reasons for it.

Rating Scale:

1	2	3	4	5
Team does not meet task requirements	Team meets most task requirements	Team meets the major task requirements	Team meets all task requirements	Team consistently exceeds expectations

102

I. *Task*

1. *Goals/Objectives*
   How well does this team establish and meet its goals/objectives?

   |_____|_____|_____|_____|_____|

   1   2   3   4   5

   Comments:

2. *Planning/Organizing*
   How well does the planning and organizing of this team prepare it to accomplish its tasks?

   |_____|_____|_____|_____|_____|

   1   2   3   4   5

   Comments:

3. *Problem Definition/Solution*
   How well does this team define and solve the problems it faces?

   |_____|_____|_____|_____|_____|

   1   2   3   4   5

   Comments:

4. *Control*
   How effective are the controls this team establishes to ensure that results are achieved as planned?

   |_____|_____|_____|_____|_____|

   1   2   3   4   5

   Comments:

5. *Follow-up*
   How well does this team follow up or take corrective action when needed?

1	2	3	4	5

Comments:

II. *Process*

   1 = Minimal teamwork conditions   5 = Ideal teamwork conditions

1. *Listening*

Members don't listen to each other and they interrupt.	All members listen and try hard to understand.

1	2	3	4	5

Comments:

2. *Communications*

Guarded, cautious.	Open, authentic.

1	2	3	4	5

Comments:

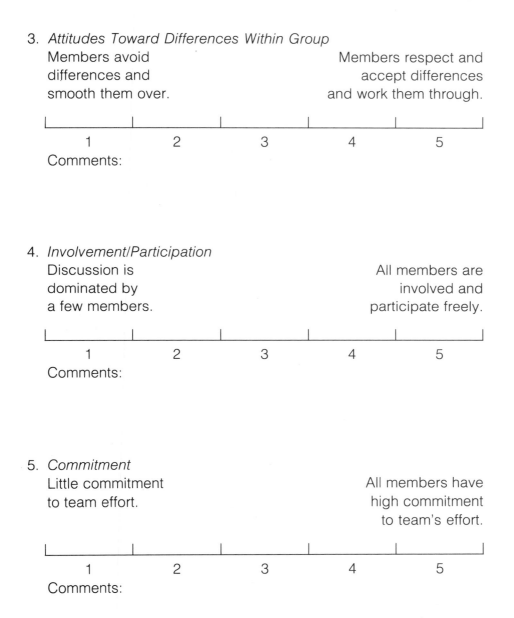

3. *Attitudes Toward Differences Within Group*

Members avoid
differences and
smooth them over.

Members respect and
accept differences
and work them through.

| 1 | 2 | 3 | 4 | 5 |

Comments:

4. *Involvement/Participation*

Discussion is
dominated by
a few members.

All members are
involved and
participate freely.

| 1 | 2 | 3 | 4 | 5 |

Comments:

5. *Commitment*

Little commitment
to team effort.

All members have
high commitment
to team's effort.

| 1 | 2 | 3 | 4 | 5 |

Comments:

6. *Mutual Support*

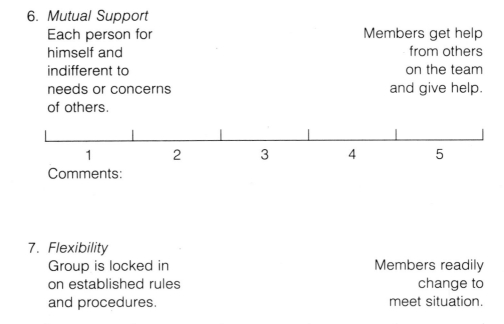

Each person for himself and indifferent to needs or concerns of others.

Members get help from others on the team and give help.

```
L_____|_____|_____|_____|_____|
      1             2            3            4            5
```

Comments:

7. *Flexibility*

Group is locked in on established rules and procedures.

Members readily change to meet situation.

```
L_____|_____|_____|_____|_____|
      1             2            3            4            5
```

Comments:

8. The team is doing the following well:

Follow-up

The best efforts at developing a team would be of little value if there is no follow-up to the team meetings on a day-to-day basis. The agreements the team reaches need to be implemented, which can be accomplished only when responsibilities are clear and people are held accountable for following up on them. Team development is not something that happens only when the team meets. It is a day-to-day activity, way of life, and way of functioning within a team.

It became obvious that follow-up was not taking place with a vice-president of distribution and his staff when at the second meeting it was learned the commitments they had made at the first meeting had not been completed. The manager had not asked people to deliver on their commitments during the interim period. Therefore, the team members did not see team development as something that happened on a daily basis but, rather, something they did on a periodic basis when they were away from the office. A discussion of this point and reinforcement by the manager of the need for follow-up resulted in team development becoming more of an ongoing, day-to-day activity for this team.

Linkage

For effective team development to take place, it is necessary to link it with other activities within the organization that will help support it. For example, most organizations reward individuals. However, they advocate teamwork. In order to get optimum teamwork, organizations will need to find ways to reward teams as well as individuals. The goal-setting management-by-objectives process of many organizations involves an individual manager setting objectives with an employee that he supervises. For effectively functioning teams, managers will need to learn how to set team goals and how to involve all members of the team so that there is understanding of and commitment to those goals. Many organizations have training programs. These training programs could greatly reinforce teamwork if they contained a module on working with and/or managing teams. The manager's job as well as the team member's job is to identify ongoing activities, programs, and systems that will help support teamwork and to determine how the team can best utilize organization resources.

The more opportunities you can find to reinforce the changes the team has decided upon, the greater the chances are that that change will be realized. Team development is no different from any other management process within the organization. It requires reinforcement, supporting systems, and, most of all, the manager's commitment to make it work.

Index